TABLE OF CONTENTS

CHAPTER	TITLE	PAGE
•	Introduction	7
1	Why Facilitation Is Necessary	10
2	What Facilitation Is (and Is Not)	15
3	Who Facilitates?	21
4	Taking Deliberate Steps	29
5	Activities to Facilitate Friendship	34
6	Getting Together After School	39
•	Conclusion	45

"Friendship is a thing most necessary to life, since without friends no one would choose to live, though possessed of all other advantages."

--- Aristotle

INTRODUCTION

Increasingly, students with disabilities who have traditionally been served in special, segregated programs are becoming full members of regular classes in their neighborhood schools. These students live in the same neighborhood with other students in the school but have had few opportunities to get to know each other. In this new arrangement, students sometimes feel uneasy about reaching out to each other, and adults feel hesitant to intervene.

Through an Innovations grant from the National Institute on Disability and Rehabilitation Research, PEAK Parent Center has explored issues about friendships which come into play when schools and communities include students who have been formerly excluded.

Connecting Students: A Guide to Thoughtful Friendship Facilitation for Educators and Families has been developed to promote reflection, dialogue, and action. It is a guide for people working to build classrooms and schools which ensure caring, acceptance, and belonging for all students.

Personal reflection exercises are included throughout the book to create opportunities for introspection, individual learning, and a means for stimulating dialogue.

Friendship facilitation is not a clearly defined process. There are qualities, attitudes, values, and skills which can be identified with successful facilitation, but there are no easy answers. Friendship facilitation is designed differently for each student.

Friendships must evolve naturally. Too much involvement in emerging friendships can frustrate their development just as humans intervening in nature can upset its delicate balance. Determining how friendships can be assisted without over-intervening is a key to successful facilitation.

As a result of our studies during this project, we are clear about the urgency of addressing this next step in inclusive education. At the same time we are hopeful having seen students develop rich relationships as a result of thoughtful facilitation.

This guide is intended to be a resource and tool for connecting students so they can develop rich, mutual friendships.

REFLECTION EXERCISE

This activity works best if you do it with a friend.

1. Complete the worksheet on the next page describing key friendships from different periods in your life.

    - List the names of several of your friends.
    - List a couple of key activities you have done with each friend.
    - Note a few key qualities that attract(ed) you to each friend.
    - Note things that you enjoy(ed) most about each person.
    - Describe where and how you met each friend.
    - Draw a symbol or picture of your relationship.

2. After you have completed the chart, answer the following questions:

    - What new insights have you gained from the first exercise?
    - Are your friends similar or different?
    - What have you and your friends enjoyed doing together?
    - Describe the significance of the symbols you drew.

3. Now consider a student with whom you are involved.

    If you were to do the chart with the student, would he have the same opportunities to meet, do things with, and enjoy the kinds of people that you have had?

    - What else can you learn from doing a chart with a student?
    - How might the chart give you ideas for facilitation?

A LOOK AT MY RELATIONSHIPS CHART

	(Friend's Name)	(Friend's Name)	(Friend's Name)
ACTIVITIES WE DID TOGETHER			
FRIENDS' KEY QUALITIES			
WHERE AND HOW WE MET			
SYMBOLS OF OUR RELATIONSHIP			

Chapter 1
Why Facilitation is Necessary

Typically, people have many different kinds of friendships, from casual acquaintances, to friends who share common activities and interests, to close friendships.

In the past, students who have disabilities and their peers who do not have had few opportunities to learn together, get to know each other in regular classes, or develop friendships beyond superficial acquaintances who say "hi" in the hall.

In addition, society has typically characterized people with disabilities as different and in need of special treatment. Children who are separated from their neighborhood schools and regular class communities for support services become isolated and "cast into roles of dependency and passivity," according to Zana Lutfiyya of Syracuse University's Center on Human Policy. Even when physically present in their school and neighborhood communities, children are often "kept at a social distance from the other members of the community."[1]

Because developing relationships requires a student's physical presence and ongoing interaction with her peers, the first step toward meeting a student's need for friendship and belonging is full school inclusion in regular classes with other students her age who live in her neighborhood. Best educational practices indicate that full inclusion with necessary supports and services brought to the student is both a possible and an effective educational model.[2]

In addition to being physically present in regular classes, students who have disabilities sometimes need added help and facilitation to make friends. According to John O'Brien and Connie Lyle O'Brien, "overcoming the social forces which push and pull people with disabilities out of community" calls for both "conscious effort" and "hard sustained work."[3] Although friendships must not be forced, positive relationships need to be intentionally facilitated in order for students with and without disabilities to get beyond the barriers and grow to know, respect, and appreciate each other as individuals.

A Contradiction: Facilitation For Friendship?

When friendship facilitation is needed, people sometimes feel hesitant because it seems unnatural and contrived. The inherent free-wheeling nature of friendship may appear to contradict the need to intentionally provide opportunities and support for positive relationships to develop among students. However, in reality, all people have to work at making friends and sometimes get help from others.

A special educator who recognizes the importance of facilitating friendships for all students says,

> *"We facilitate for each other every day in our personal lives. When my friend who is also a teacher went to England as part of a teacher exchange program, she asked me to introduce and support the teacher who was taking her place. I introduced the British teacher to my friends and soon a whole network developed around her to make her feel welcome and to support her through the school year. Because she was alone in a new country, she had "special needs" which required facilitation and support. We as educators need to transfer this to our work in schools and recognize that our students have the same needs that we have."*[4]

Another teacher relates,

> *"I was introduced to my husband by a friend who set us up on a blind date. She and I taught in the same school and her husband*

and my future spouse worked for the same business. My husband was very shy and hesitant about meeting me at first. My friend got four tickets to a concert and invited both of us to go along with her husband and her. With the facilitation and support of the other couple, we really hit it off, found out we had much in common, and after a few years, we got married."[5]

Recognizing the role friendship facilitation and support play in their own lives helps educators realize the need for intentionality in helping all students make friends.

Importance of Friendships For Everyone

The need for positive relationships and for friends is universal. Schools are currently increasing their focus on students' relationships as a crucial aspect of learning. The need for friendships and belonging is being addressed by school restructuring leaders to better meet all students' needs. In the book, *Improving Schools from Within*, Roland Barth states, "What needs to be improved about schools is their culture, the quality of interpersonal relationships, and the nature and quality of learning experiences."[6] Schools must become caring communities. In fact, Elliot Eisner lists this as one of the six essential components of "what really counts" in schools.[7] Marsha Forest believes that friendships and relationships are preconditions for learning in schools.[8]

As educators focus on the role relationships play in educating the whole child, it becomes clear that all aspects of a student's development are interdependent and must be integrated in order for learning to be meaningful to the student. Special education has traditionally approached students' learning according to domains (social needs, communication needs, academic needs, etc.). Regular education typically has isolated specific subject or "content" areas (reading, math, social studies, etc.). Both of these practices frequently fragment students' school experiences. Douglas Biklen points out that "students' social and emotional well-being ...cannot be dissociated from academic achievement."[9] According to Alfie Kohn, "the development of perspective-taking - the capacity to imagine how someone else thinks, feels, or sees the world - tends to promote cognitive problem solving."[10]

William Glasser indicates that one reason many students have behavioral challenges is because the school is not satisfying basic needs to belong and love, to gain power, to be free, and to have fun. When students show challenging behaviors, they are communicating important information about their unmet needs. The needs for belonging, freedom, and fun are satisfied through social relationships and friendships. In addition, Glasser's research with high school students found that students' perceptions about their own self-worth were defined through their social contacts rather than through their academic achievement. In fact, when asked why they attend school, many high school students list their friends as a primary reason.[11] All students - no matter how significant the challenges they present to schools - must have opportunities and encouragement to develop friendships.

Frequently educators view relationships as secondary to a student's education; but when they view friendships as primary conditions for a caring, constructive learning environment, all students do better and learn more. ■

REFLECTION EXERCISE

1. Friendships are important for all children. Think about a child or teenager whom you care about and know well. This can be your own child or the child of a close relative or friend.

2. Describe the importance of this young person having friends and feeling that she belongs in her school and neighborhood community.

3. How will friendship opportunities and a sense of belonging make a difference in this student's growth in academics as well as in other areas and future success?

4. What are ways that this student's teachers can help him to feel part of the school and to make positive connections with other students?

5. What can this young person's parents and family do to help her make friends and feel that she belongs?

Chapter 2
What Facilitation Is (And Is Not)

Friendships cannot be forced. However, facilitation can assist students to get to know each other. Because people frequently notice differences before similarities, a facilitator who shows students that a classmate with disabilities has feelings, interests, and experiences in common with them can trigger new relationships for students with and without disabilities.

What Facilitation Is

Zana Lutfiyya has defined friendship facilitation as: "providing opportunities where people can comfortably come together to meet each other."[12] Facilitation is people accepting responsibility to ensure that a student is connected to his or her peers and has encouragement, opportunities, and assistance to develop all sorts of relationships - including close, deep friendships. Facilitation is an unobtrusive process which taps the expertise of others who know the student well and allows the student to choose the friends with whom she wants to develop relationships. Facilitators are there to help the process along when needed by inviting students to get to know each other, encouraging budding relationships, modeling ways to include the student, and getting out of the way as friendships develop.

Lutfiyya has identified three kinds of facilitation activities which help people build connections that lead to friendships. They are finding opportunities, interpretation, and accommodation.[13]

Finding Opportunities

Finding opportunities involves **performing actions that help to bring students together.** It can involve a wide range of strategies from finding or planning opportunities for students to providing actual individualized support in order to enable a student to participate with peers.

John, a special education teacher who acts as a facilitator for a high school student with challenging needs, makes it his responsibility to be aware of what's happening socially in the school. John arranges details and determines accommodations and supports which ensure Randy's active participation in classroom activities and after-school activities like dances, club projects, etc. In addition to attending the homecoming dance with his date, Randy was on the student team which planned the event, chose the refreshments, and decorated the gym.

Interpretation

Interpretation is **presenting a person to others in a positive and enhancing way**. Interpreting a student with disabilities to other students and adults in ways that highlight the student's strengths and gifts is important because it draws people together.

Sheila, who provides support for a sixth grade student who cannot communicate with others in conventional ways because of his disability, sees helping students understand that they ***can*** *communicate with him as one of her primary objectives. "I try to find opportunities for him to show them that he can hear and understand and that it's his muscles that don't work," she states.*

Mark finds opportunities where Tom can highlight his strengths to his high school classmates and teachers in his participation in class and school activities. For example, when Tom was having trouble during band practice when the percussionists were not involved, Mark suggested that Tom become a media assistant since he is good at running tape recorders and video cameras. Tom assumed responsibility for taping and replaying musical segments for the band to use to critique themselves and improve their performance.

Emily's mother says that because Emily is outgoing and gregarious, she does a lot of her own positive interpretation to other students.

Adults in the school assist the process by staying out of the way. When they don't intervene, the message to Emily's peers is that she is capable and okay as a friend.

Representing the student with disabilities in a positive way may be the most significant component of supporting friendships. Modeling by adults is a subtle but highly powerful variable. Debbie Quick, a classroom teacher, states, "Teachers are influential role models for all kids. We must consider everything we do and say carefully."[14]

■ Accommodations

Accommodations are **the actual changes or adaptations in the physical environment which help to involve an individual in some way**. A student may need specific adaptations or accommodations in order to participate with peers so that positive relationships can begin and flourish. Several examples of accommodations follow.

When the P.E. class did jumping jacks, Wilson, who uses a wheelchair, moved only his arms in rhythm with the exercises. "I look at it like having a broken leg and adapt," says the teacher. "Any kid can have a broken leg."

Michael, a middle school student who is deaf, likes his math class because his teacher always writes clear instructions on the board to help Michael stay in touch with what's happening. The teacher also provides a helpful accommodation by having Michael's friend, Jimmy, sit in the desk in front of Michael. Since Michael is taller, he still has a clear view of the teacher and can read the teacher's lips easily. Jimmy is perceptive as to when Michael is not comprehending information and lets the teacher know.

For a marketing club competition, Janet, a speech therapist, made visual cue cards to help a student participate in consumer/salesperson role plays.

Facilitation Is Individualized

Friendship facilitation is a highly personalized process, and activities look different for each student. In addition, the amount of facilitation a student needs is determined by each individual activity. Decisions on facilitation strategies are made by considering the unique characteristics of the students involved - their likes, dislikes, interests, strengths, and personalities.

Phillip needed work in sign language to communicate more effectively and to better comprehend academic materials. However, he did not feel comfortable being singled out to be tutored in sign. Instead, his teacher (with consultation from the special education staff) incorporated sign language as a part of the regular language arts curriculum for all students in the class. Now, the entire class is enhancing its language skills and viewing signing in a positive light.

A second grader, who needed assistance to learn how to get along with peers on the playground, liked being independent and responded negatively when adults or other students hovered over her telling her what to do. The paraprofessional assigned to support Jenee on the playground honored her desire for independence by remaining in the background and letting her choose what she wanted to do and who she interacted with. Nonetheless, she was available to interpret Jenee positively to others and help her better understand challenging situations if they arose.

What Facilitation Is Not

Some practices commonly used in schools that are thought to help students develop relationships may actually divert friendship facilitation efforts. Although these activities may be useful for other reasons, they sometimes set students with disabilities apart by focusing on their "specialness" or differences.

Facilitation is not choosing a best friend for a student, assigning a peer tutor, or grouping two vulnerable students. Facilitation is also not a social skills curriculum, a weekly friendship club in a classroom, disability awareness activities, or a credit program for honors students to spend time with a student with disabilities.

To a society which tends to view friendships between people with disabilities and those without as traditional volunteer relationships where one person needs a friend for support and the other person is only there to help the individual with the disability, these approaches may appear to be logical means of promoting positive relationships. However, although well-intentioned, these practices may promote one-sided, helping relationships or make the development of mutually satisfying relationships difficult.

Programs or approaches like those described above cannot automatically or effectively meet individual students' needs for friendship and belonging. Beane's research shows that "direct instruction in course-like settings does not produce lasting or strong effects in the affective domain."[15] Addressing friendship support by implementing special programs may actually diminish the importance of friendship for students with disabilities by reducing it to the status of an isolated learning objective among many other components of the curriculum. First-hand experiences in a one-to-one, mutual relationship are more effective in helping students develop friends.

Therefore, facilitation is an individualized process in which adults assume responsibility for assisting students with disabilities to be connected and have all sorts of opportunities for rich, diverse friendships. It is a process in which students with disabilities are viewed in terms of their strengths and the contributions they will make in relationships. The message is that all students are givers *and* receivers and can develop mutual friendships. ■

REFLECTION EXERCISE

Reflecting again on your personal experiences of friendship, do the following exercise.

1. Consider this story:

   Mary has just moved to town with her husband and children. Her only acquaintance in town is Janet, a close friend from high school. Before they moved, Mary called Janet who was excited about renewing their friendship. Janet looks forward to introducing Mary to her community and friends.

   a. What are some ways that Janet can help Mary get to know people?

   b. Janet knew Mary's positive qualities as well as her shortcomings. Why is it important for Janet to highlight Mary's strengths and interests when introducing her to others? How can Janet interpret her in a positive way to others?

2. Think about all the ways that you have facilitated relationships for people you know. (Think of activities like setting up blind dates, introducing people who you think would enjoy each other, etc.)

3. How have you interpreted a friend to someone else in a positive way?

4. How have you made accommodations so that a friend could participate in an activity with you? How has a friend made an accommodation for you? (Consider things like skiing on the "less than expert" slopes with a friend who is less skilled even though you enjoy more difficult ones.)

Chapter 3
Who Facilitates?

Who is responsible for friendship facilitation? When it is determined that support is needed to facilitate friendships for a particular student, no one person can be solely in charge. Instead, the responsibility is shared by everyone involved with the student. Assumptions about who should facilitate are sometimes made based on traditionally accepted roles of school personnel and common school practices. However, persons experienced in friendship facilitation efforts state the importance of flexibility and innovation when determining who should facilitate.

All people who know the student need to be involved in creatively exploring opportunities and strategies for facilitating friendships throughout the student's life. The role is shared by regular educators, teacher aides, classmates, family members, special educators, therapists, counselors, and community people who know the student well and are committed to her long-term success and happiness.

Maria's planning team was concerned that her emotional disability was a barrier to being accepted as a friend by other students in her first grade class. They determined that friendship facilitation for Maria needed to be shared by several members of the team.

- *The first grade and special education teachers co-taught a weekly journal writing session in which students expressed their feelings. This activity provided opportunities to address all the students' needs for social and behavioral support - not just Maria's.*
- *The district behavior consultant met with the teachers every other week to help plan activities for the journal session as well as problem-solve specific behavioral issues.*

- *The school's principal, who often visited classrooms, complimented Maria on an accomplishment whenever he came into the first grade class.*

Keisha's classmates seemed to be overly preoccupied with tattling when she misbehaved on the playground. Pat, a school psychologist who is part of Keisha's planning team, suggested to the teacher that she encourage the students to report only good things that they catch each other doing when they come in from recess. Pat's intervention turned the situation around, stopped the challenging behaviors, and helped all of the students in the class to see each other in a more positive light.

When schools use a collaborative model for meeting all students' needs, the roles of the various individuals in the school become fluid and not as traditionally defined. For instance, a teacher may be very good at figuring out accommodations or determining activities which bring students together but not feel adept in supporting the actual interactions between students. Therefore, one individual may feel comfortable with some aspects of facilitation and not with others. The challenge is for the team to ensure that staff view their responsibilities broadly so that students' needs for facilitation are met well.

Students -- The Best Facilitators

In classrooms which promote friendship and belonging as a necessary component of the regular curriculum, students naturally become facilitators for each other. Students are the experts who are most perceptive about each other's feelings, needs, and interests. They know more about their age-group's "culture" and can communicate that more effectively than adults can. Students also typically have much more influence over each other than adults do.

Another important quality is a student's ability to put a classmate's needs into a balanced perspective with the needs and experiences all kids have in common.

A parent who was picking up his son at the end of a week at a Boy Scout camp observed his son and a boy with severe disabilities interacting as they took down their tents to pack up. On the way home, the father asked his son to tell him about the other boy, expecting to hear his son's perspectives on the young man's disability. Instead, the boy's reply was, "Boy, does he hate oatmeal." The parent says, "It seemed apparent to me at that point that good 'boy to boy' things had happened at the camp and that I need not expect or push anything else at the time."[16]

Adults tend to intellectualize about problems to the point where solutions seem much more complex than they actually are. However, students help to keep the focus on what really makes sense for their peers. Involving students in determining how to support each other's unique needs as part of the class routine is an important strategy. Also, many planning teams have found that involving peers to determine supports and facilitation strategies for their classmates with disabilities is a highly effective practice.

Qualities For Successful Facilitation

People experienced in helping students become connected have identified specific qualities as important for people who are involved in connecting students. They made statements about some of these qualities:

OPENNESS TO DEVELOPING AN ONGOING, POSITIVE RELATIONSHIP WITH THE STUDENT

"Adults who have been most successful with Emily have not had the "helper" mentality. They begin with the belief that she is a 100% citizen. They accept and like her for who she is, and because of that, the support they offer is very natural."

SKILL IN INVITING STUDENTS TO BE FRIENDS

"Becka, a student with *significant needs, is a member of my kindergarten class. Whenever I get a new student I introduce the student to each member of the class by name.*

When I introduce Becka I explain that she talks to us in a different way and I ask her to show us how she raises her eyes to say 'Yes'. After Becka demonstrates her method of communication, I have the class practice responding to my questions using Becka's communication system. This models for the new student and for the whole class that Becka is an important part of the class and facilitates acceptance, belonging, and friendship for her."

AN UNDERSTANDING OF HOW OTHER STUDENTS THIS AGE MAKE FRIENDS AND SPEND TIME TOGETHER IN THE NEIGHBORHOOD AND SCHOOL

"Sean is a good facilitator because he helps with the track team, so he knows what the kids are up to after school."

FLEXIBILITY

"You can't have a tight game plan. You've got to let the kids make choices. You never know where a day might be headed. Problems arise which must be solved. People with different personalities and viewpoints must be accommodated."

ABILITY TO PROBLEM SOLVE CREATIVELY

"This takes active participation from everyone involved and that's hard sometimes. When we meet, sometimes a teacher says, 'But, I don't see how he can participate in this activity,' and expects me to have the answers. I have to encourage her to problem-solve by saying, 'What would work best for you? How do you think you can include him?'"

PERSEVERANCE

"It's really important not to give up. There's always an answer. If there's not an answer, then you're failing, not the kids, because you're not trying to figure out a way to make it work."

COMFORT IN BEING UNOBTRUSIVE

"This is the most important quality; this is the key. When you're facilitating, you're not there to be in the spotlight; you're there to assist only where assistance is needed. I get my satisfaction from seeing the kids and the other adults taking the initiative and interacting with David and

supporting him in a natural way. I feel like I'm doing my job when he is given a part in the school play, when he does a good job independently, and when I see him playing with a group of kids on the playground."

ORIENTATION TOWARDS THE STUDENT'S STRENGTHS

"We helped Rob learn a drum solo for the senior talent show. In spite of his significant intellectual disability, his good sense of rhythm and experience as a member of the percussion section of the band really showed. He's well-liked and quite a 'showman.' He put on a great performance."

Finding the Right People to Facilitate

Students with disabilities are sometimes provided with extra physical and or academic support from teachers' assistants. There is often an assumption made that these paraprofessionals are the best choice to serve in the role of connecting students. This can sometimes be a faulty assumption. Although an individual may be very good at physical assistance, or at assisting a student to successfully participate in academic activities, the same person should not automatically be assumed to be the best or only person to facilitate friendships. When determining who should fill facilitation roles, team members should keep in mind the qualities listed above.

A regular education teacher whose class includes a student with significant challenges relates why she chose a particular woman, the energetic mother of three sons, from the available candidates for the job of supporting the student in her classroom. She states, "I knew she (the support person) would get him in the middle of whatever was going on in the classroom". [17] This teacher's intuitive sense about the person's qualifications communicates an important message about criteria for choosing appropriate people to provide facilitation for students.

Julie, an adult who provides friendship facilitation for Mark, a student with significant physical disabilities, introduces herself as "Mark's sidekick." She doesn't present herself to staff or other kids as the "expert" directly responsible for Mark. She's there to give him assistance - only when it's needed - so that he can participate actively in sixth grade. She lets Mark and the other kids call the shots.

Another important criteria is to choose people who "fit in well" with the students. Julie happens to be young, energetic, and the kids think she's "cool." Since she fits in well with the students, these qualities lessen the possibility that Julie will intrude upon the typical interactions and culture of students of that age. As Mark moves on, he, his fellow students and his planning team think that finding male facilitators will be important for junior high.

Sometimes a specific individual called an "integration facilitator" is designated to coordinate the inclusion of a student. This person does not take full responsibility for facilitating for the student, but synchronizes the efforts of everyone else involved with the student. The integration facilitator becomes a kind of "relationship coordinator." It is essential that a facilitator's role be determined carefully to ensure that she/he does not get in the way of a student's independence or the development of natural relationships and supports.[18]

When planning who will provide a student's facilitation, many factors should be considered. Above all, a student's facilitators must have a positive relationship with the student, an understanding of the goals of facilitation, a commitment to the process, and the skill to facilitate without getting in the way. ■

REFLECTION EXERCISE

Identify a student with whom you are involved who has challenging needs and is included in a regular class.

1. List the names of the people who currently participate on the student's planning team and others who might participate who know the student well and who may have valuable insight or abilities.

   Current Participants ______________________________

   ____

   ____

   Possible Participants ______________________________

   ____

   ____

2. Based on each team member's individual strengths, interests, relationships with the student, and expertise, identify the person from the above lists who might best facilitate friendships for the student in the following activities:

   Recess or free periods ________________

   An after-school activity ________________
   (like a club meeting or sports event)

   Classroom learning center activities ________________

   An informal class discussion ________________

continued . . .

An overnight field trip ____________

Lunchtime in the cafeteria ____________

A Valentine's Dance ____________

Literature class ____________

A science lab ____________

3. As a member of this student's planning team, evaluate yourself according to the following qualities for successful facilitation. Indicate whether the quality is one you already have or one you need to develop or refine.

a) Openness to developing ongoing, positive relationship with student

ALREADY HAVE NEED TO WORK ON

b) Skill in inviting others to be friends

ALREADY HAVE NEED TO WORK ON

c) Flexibility

ALREADY HAVE NEED TO WORK ON

d) Creative problem-solving ability

ALREADY HAVE NEED TO WORK ON

e) Perseverance

ALREADY HAVE NEED TO WORK ON

f) Comfort being in the background

ALREADY HAVE NEED TO WORK ON

g) Orientation to focusing on student's strengths

ALREADY HAVE NEED TO WORK ON

Chapter 4
Taking Deliberate Steps

What steps can be taken to facilitate relationships? It is impossible to prescribe a specific set of strategies, but people who have experience connecting students offer the following practical guidelines.

1. **Step back and survey the situation.**
   Look at the big picture before making any decisions:

   - How "connected" with other students is the student with disabilities? Is he lonely? Does he have acquaintances with other students in school? Do school friendships carry over to after-school phone calls, invitations to parties, or neighborhood play activities?

   - Pay close attention to the student's behavior and what he/she may be communicating. Who is she drawn to? What activities does he appear to enjoy? When is she happy? Not happy? Why might he be acting the way he is?

   - Be aware that challenging behavior can be communication of a student's unmet needs for belonging and friendships.

2. **Review the student's day.**

   - Friendships and belonging must be encouraged and nurtured across all activities and encounters in any student's day. Therefore, in targeting friendship facilitation opportunities, don't limit them to the commonly accepted school "socialization" activities like recess, lunch, and sports activities. Include classroom and after school activities as well.

3. Estimate how much facilitation will be needed.

- The degree of facilitation and support required by a student (or by the other students who might become her friends) depends on those students' individual needs, the particular culture of the classroom and school, and the type of activity. For example, during a video in class, students might need much less facilitation than during lunchtime in the cafeteria.

- For some students, facilitation may be necessary only at certain times, like the beginning of the school year or during transitions to a new school. Other students may require ongoing facilitation to initiate and build friendships.

- The culture in classrooms and the school is a significant variable in determining the amount and types of facilitation needed. The age and the gender of the students are additional factors.

- In school environments where there is a culture of caring and where all students have goals for self-esteem and getting along with others infused throughout the regular curriculum, friendships and belonging are natural outcomes. In these settings, there may be less need for individual facilitation.

Important rule: ensure that facilitation efforts are not overdone. Typically providing the least amount of adult presence possible is a good rule of thumb.

4. **Determine the type(s) of facilitation which will be most helpful.**

   - The three kinds of facilitation described in Chapter 2 (finding opportunities, interpretation, and accommodation) can provide a basis for friendship facilitation activities. *Finding opportunities* for potential relationships to develop is an important component. As students become involved in activities with each other, positive *interpretation* of the student with disabilities to her classmates and potential friends is often helpful. *Accommodations* which enable him to participate actively may be needed in varying degrees based on the particular student and situation.

5. **Decide upon specific facilitation activities which will be helpful for the particular student at the time.**

   See Chapter 5 for examples of facilitation activities.

6. **Identify the person(s) who can best provide the needed facilitation.**

   - The answer to the question, "Who facilitates?" is "Whoever is the most logical person at the given time and in the particular situation for this student."

   - Instead of designating one friendship facilitator and assigning all responsibilities to that person, whoever stands out as having the necessary skills or qualities as described in Chapter 3 should be involved in facilitation. Often, the best facilitators emerge from the student's classmates.

   - It is important to structure things so that it does not appear that only one adult is capable of interacting with and facilitating for a particular student. Many people in many different ways - teachers designing their curriculum and classroom environment, a principal interacting with students in the lunchroom, a teacher assistant lending physical support to a student during an after school activity, and friends of the student - can be effective facilitators.

7. **Explore ways to use the regular curriculum to teach values about diversity, equality, and friendships.**

    - An English literature teacher whose class included a student with significant disabilities examined *Romeo and Juliet* in terms of how prejudices and stereotypes can get in the way of the development of friendships. Following the discussion, the class strategized ways to fully include the student with disabilities in class activities so that she could feel that she belonged. Other students then began to see her as a potential friend and know her for her strengths and shared interests which helped friendships to develop.

8. **Use teaching techniques that promote cooperation and equality among students.**

    - Use a variety of instructional methods which allow a student with disabilities to participate actively and meaningfully in regular class activities and promote a cooperative classroom environment.

    - Examples of these instructional techniques are: cooperative learning, hands-on activities, experience-based instruction, class projects, demonstrations, and role-playing.

    - An added advantage is that these same instructional techniques promote more meaningful and active learning for all students.

9. **Assess the situation frequently. When something is not working, try a different strategy.**

   - Use creative strategizing and commit to making things work. Monitor the student's active participation. When challenges arise, assume that solutions exist. Evaluate and re-strategize continually to develop new, more successful plans. View challenges as opportunities to discover better ways of doing things.

10. **Withdraw adult presence as soon as possible.**

    - It is important in any friendship facilitation efforts NOT to assume that specific adult intervention will always be needed. The goal must be to phase out adults' presence as natural relationships and supports emerge. Then adults' roles change to monitoring how things are going and implementing "behind the scenes" facilitation as needed.

REFLECTION EXERCISE

1. What is your personal reaction to the facilitation process described in Chapter 4?

2. What parts of this process have you used in the past?

3. How is using this process different from implementing programs designed to teach social skills or acceptance of students with disabilities?

Chapter 5
Activities To Facilitate Friendshi

As shown in the previous chapter, friendship facilitation is a process. Because of this, there are no "cookbook" answers for how to facilitate. Facilitation strategies must be individually determined and are based on a multitude of variables, such as the individual needs of the students, the personalities of the students and adults involved, the age and gender of the students, and the culture of the classroom and the school.

Following are some activities which persons experienced in facilitating friendships have used.

- **Give the student valued roles in cooperative learning groups and other class activities (assigning her tasks in which she can show-off her strengths).**

- **Tell the student's classmates about his special interests and talents.**

- **Use strategies for dealing with a student's challenging behaviors which teach the class positive social or coping skills rather than singling out the student with disabilities.**

- **Be available to demonstrate support strategies, answer questions, interpret communication, and address concerns.**

- **Assist classmates in understanding a student's communication by modeling and encouraging them to communicate with him directly.**

- **Encourage honest communication about concerns, fears, questions, and issues that arise.**

- **Hold regular class discussions about friendship and belonging.** (*eg. How can we support each other and help each other feel welcome and important in the class especially at the beginning of the year and when a new student arrives?)*

- **Offer encouragement and praise for positive efforts of adults and students.**

- **Invite classmates to assist in planning facilitation strategies for the student.**

- **Encourage adults and students involved to get together to figure things out when challenges arise.**

- **Reflect the belief that problems can be solved and can create new opportunities for growth.**

- **Provide opportunities for students to honestly identify their strengths and needs.** *(Discuss how class members can highlight strengths and support each other.)*

- **Assist students and families to build friendships after school.** *(See Chapter 6 for information on strategies schools and families can use to facilitate friendships which extend beyond school.)*

The Circle of Friends

When a more intense and individualized facilitation strategy seems necessary, building a support circle for a student can be a means of helping students with and without disabilities develop friendships. Forest and Lusthaus describe the "circle of friends" as "a network that allows for the genuine involvement of children in a friendship, caring, and support role with their peers".[19] In order to be successful and lasting, the circle of friends concept must be used as an ongoing process. Forest cautions that "the Circles...technique may become routinized in schools and possibly detract from teachers' and students' efforts to develop more natural forms of support and friendship."[20]

Any relationships must be nurtured, supported, and reinforced in order to flourish. Interpretation and accommodation may be necessary components at various stages in the process.

No matter the activity, constant adult presence poses a problem for students. Douglas Biklen states that a student can become "isolated from others in the class because he or she is constantly in the presence of a teaching aide. He goes on to note that "an aide may unintentionally become a chaperone or the person's only companion."[21] Constant adult presence keeps peers from learning to communicate directly with the student and reinforces a perception that the student does not share interests or have needs similar to the other students'.

The friendship facilitation activities offered in this chapter are a small sampling of what is possible. When teams of educators and families come together with the common goal of supporting friendships and belonging for students with disabilities and for all students, the possibilities are limitless. Facilitation plans are most successful when they are customized for a particular student, his or her team of adults, and the school, family, and neighborhood community.

INTERPRETATION - A CRITICAL ELEMENT

- Is encouraging friendships among all students (not just focusing on the student with disabilities) a goal in the class?"
- Do the adults involved show that all children are equally valued and respected through every word uttered and every action taken?
- Are all children spoken to in the same manner, tone of voice, etc.?
- Are all children treated age-appropriately?
- Do adults intentionally find ways to highlight each child's strengths for the rest of the class?
- Do adults reflect that they, themselves, are totally comfortable with all the children (even in potentially "uncomfortable" situations, like behavioral challenges, feeding, toileting, etc.)?
- Do adults promote a fun and friendly classroom atmosphere to help the children feel at ease with each other.[22]

REFLECTION EXERCISE

1. List strengths and interests for the student with disabilities you identified earlier. Consult with the student, his/her classmates, and others who know the student well to make additions to your list.

2. Identify and list interests, hobbies, likes, dislikes, etc. of some of this student's classmates. Talk with others (including the students themselves) to compile this information.

3. List the regular class schedule as well as other activities in a typical day (before, during, and after school) for the students. Then, identify and circle all of the potential opportunities for the student to interact with classmates during a typical day.

4. Using the list of facilitation activities from this chapter, find five strategies which you have used in the past to support the student. (You can also list strategies not included in the list which you have found to be successful.)

5. Now identify five strategies which you will use soon or which you will encourage a classmate or another team member to use to facilitate friendship.

Chapter 6
Getting Together After School

Typically, friendships which begin in school carry over for students after school. Some examples are described below.

A group of third graders get together after school to ride bikes around the neighborhood and then go back to one kid's house to play Nintendo.

A kindergarten student invites several friends to her house to play on a Saturday afternoon.

A group of high school students go together to the basketball game and then out for pizza afterwards.

A fifth grade girl has a slumber party for her birthday and invites some friends from her class.

An eighth grade boy whose dad received extra tickets to the professional football playoffs invites several of his school friends to go along.

Several sophomore girls go together shopping and to a movie at the mall.

Opportunities like these are taken for granted by the parents and educators of most children. However, students with disabilities are often deprived of and yet desperately need these same opportunities. Sometimes educators and parents fail to address the important link that exists between the formation of relationships in school and opportunities for involvement in after-school and weekend activities with a student's neighborhood peers. The unfortunate result is that many students with disabilities, even though they have classmates who interact with them at school, are isolated and lonely after school and lack experiences of true, mutual friendship.

One mother says,

> *"My son's classmates still see him as "special" and don't automatically consider him when they're planning after-school activities. They assume that he is not interested in or capable of participating. They sometimes judge that his father and I think he needs to be near us all of the time for protection and support. Although he is popular with his classmates at school, he leads a very lonely, isolated life after school with few friends and outside activities."*[23]

Even when schools provide activities during the school day to connect and support students with unique challenges, intentional efforts must be made to build opportunities for students so that friendships develop which extend beyond the classroom and school. Facilitation of these friendships requires a joint effort between school and home.

Families and schools express different perspectives about who is responsible for facilitation after school hours. Parents report that when they ask the school for help, they are told that friendships are what happen after school and are the parents' responsibility. Sometimes schools state that they can't be involved in sharing names of classmates with families because of confidentiality. However, one father states, "We don't know who our son spends time with, who's in his classes, or who he particularly likes at school. How can we reach out to encourage friendships on our own?"[24] In order for families to be able to assist students with disabilities to develop relationships which carry over after school, families must have information about what happens at school.

What Schools Can Do

Educators and families must assume joint responsibility for ensuring that a student has genuine friends in her life. For educators, this means actively involving the student's family in planning and decision-making for the student. Maintaining open and frequent communication with families is an important key. Sharing information about budding relationships, problem-solving about obstacles that arise, and offering each other ideas for how potential friendships can be promoted and supported both at school and at home is beneficial for everyone.

Ben's augmentative communication specialist always pulled in his friends when she came into the classroom to work on the computer with Ben. When she came to Ben's home at the beginning of the summer as part of his Extended School Year services, she encouraged his family to invite some of the same students to come over as well to work on the computer. This became the start of weekly "get-togethers" for the group at Ben's house. The therapist states, "I was pushed out of the way very quickly, and the kids taught each other incredible things."[25]

Other ways that schools can provide friendship support links between school, home, and community are by encouraging and supporting students' involvement in extra curricular activities like art, dance, or drama classes, band, after school choir, sporting events, and school clubs.

In addition, schools can inform parents about community recreation opportunities and encourage the students to join. School people need also to tell parents the particular activities that friends of the student are interested in. "There are so many resources in the community, and people at school can take initiative to introduce these ideas to parents," states a special educator.[26]

What Families Can Do

When parents are in touch with the school, they can facilitate after-school activities for their child with students from his class. When families are made aware of emerging school friendships, parents can assist their children to invite peers to their home to watch videos, play, participate in family outings, attend birthday parties, and do other activities. Friendships made at home can then carry back into school as well and help a child feel welcome and secure there.

Families can also access typical community resources that their child's schoolmates use day-to-day. For instance, scouting is an activity in which all children can participate and enjoy outside of school. Community recreation and park programs offer activities after school, on weekends, and during summer vacations. Accessing other community resources such as church or synagogue youth groups, YMCA recreation programs, museum or library enrichment classes, or youth bowling leagues are steps families can take.

A family whose son had previously attended only segregated summer camps for children with disabilities enrolled their child in the regular YMCA camp. Their initial apprehensions gave way to positive feelings at the end of the week when they saw the tremendous benefit of their child's presence at the camp both to him and the other campers.[27]

A key in deciding which avenues to pursue is observing the child's classmates from school and scheduling one's own child in the same activities.

One parent shares, "At first we were fearful when approaching these generic community groups to get our daughter involved. But, for the most part, we have been impressed with how open and supportive people have been about her participation. It's so easy when she's with her friends."[28]

An additional role for parents is to moniter if and how friendships are developing for their son or daughter. Particularly as students get older than elementary age, parents' roles change. It can be awkward and stigmatizing for a student to have one's parent along on a trip with friends to the movies, mall, or a friend's house.

Who Provides Facilitation After School?

Facilitation for a student with special needs can often be provided by the organization sponsoring the recreational activity if parents assist with preparation and modeling prior to the activity.

The staff at a park and recreation day camp discovered that they were able to assist a child who uses a wheelchair to participate in rugged and interactive camp activities after his parents spent some time instructing them about their child's support and communication needs.[29]

Since many supports a child may require (e.g., transportation, interpreter for sign language, friendship facilitation, etc.) are not automatically provided in community activities as they are during the school day, parents sometimes arrange for supports on their own. Some families hire a teenager to facilitate the child's involvement. Or parents request that a person who has connected the student at school be asked to "consult" or help out in some way. In addition, parents use their child's Extended School Year plan, and the school district provides facilitation in summer or after school activities. Family members can also volunteer as advisers, sponsors, or helpers for activities.

A successful strategy that parents report is signing the child up for activities with a friend from school who knows the child well. The friend can then participate with, model supports, and advocate for his or her buddy. It is important to note that if friends from school participate together in activities, frequently a formal adult support person is not needed. The end result is that the more that students are able to interact outside school, the more easily they relate and are genuinely connected in their schools and communities.

REFLECTION EXERCISE

NOTE: It is important that school staff as well as parents do this exercise.

1. Describe some of the efforts you have already made to facilitate friendships with classmates outside of school time for your student.

2 What efforts will you now make to facilitate friendships with classmates after school? Consider the activities the student might enjoy. Remember to capitalize on her strengths and interests.

3. What are the most difficult aspects for you in assisting students through facilitating friendships outside of school time?

4. Who are some other people in the student's network who might be good resources for you?

CONCLUSION

Relationships are critical for everyone. Students with disabilities are often left out because adults aren't sure how to assist them to develop relationships and also don't want to intrude on what is perceived to be a natural process. This book attempts to reflect current thinking from people actively engaged in this process of assisting students with disabilities to become connected. Since this is a relatively new area for people to think about, new thoughts, understanding, and ideas are constantly emerging. It is essential that people facilitating friendships continue to learn from the process. Above all, deliberate reflection coupled with action are essential so that ALL students have opportunities for plentiful, rich relationships in their lives.

"The only way to have a friend is to be one."

END NOTES

[1] Lutfiyya, Z. M. (1988). *Reflections on Relationships Between People with Disabilities and Typical People.* Syracuse, NY: The Center on Human Policy. 19pp.

[2] Sailor, W. (1990). Community School: An Essay. In L. Meyer, C. Peck, & L. Brown (Eds.). Critical Issues in the Lives of People with Severe Disabilities. Baltimore: Paul H. Brookes; Schnorr, R. F. (1990). Peter, He Comes and Goes. *Journal of the Association for Persons with Severe Handicaps*, 15(4), 231-240; Stainback, S. & Stainback, W. (1988). Educating Students with Severe Disabilities. *Teaching Exceptional Children*, 21(1), 16-19.

[3] O'Brien, J. & Lyle O'Brien, C. (1991). *Members of Each Other: Perspectives on Social Support for People with Severe Disabilities.* Lithonia, GA: Responsive Systems Associates.

[4] Bartolo, M. (1992). Personal communication.

[5] Dillard, B. (1992). Personal communication.

[6] Barth, R. (1990). *Improving Schools From Within: Teachers, Parents, and Principals Can Make the Difference.* San Francisco: Jossey-Bass Inc. Publishers.

[7] Eisner, E. (1991, February). What Really Counts in Schools. *Educational Leadership*, 10-17.

[8] Forest, M.(1990, February). *MAPS and circles.* Presentation at PEAK Parent Center Workshop, Colorado Springs.

[9] Biklen, D. (1989). Making Differences Ordinary. In S. Stainback, W. Stainback, & M. Forest (Eds.). *Educating All Students in the Mainstream of Regular Education.* Baltimore: Paul H. Brookes.

[10] Kohn, A. (1991, March). Caring Kids: The Role of Schools, *Phi Delta Kappan*, 497-506.

[11] Glasser, W. (1986). *Control Theory in the Classroom.* New York: Harper & Row Publishers, Inc.

[12] Lutfiyya, Z. M. (1988). *Reflections on Relationships Between People With Disabilities and Typical People.* Syracuse, NY: Syracuse University,The Center On Human Policy. 19pp.

[13] Lutfiyya, Z. M. (1990). *Tony Santi and the Bakery: The Roles of Facilitation, Accommodation, and Interpretation.* Syracuse, NY: Syracuse University, The Center On Human Policy. 14 pp.

[14] Quick, D. (1991). Personal communication.

[15] Beane, J. A. (1991, September). Sorting Out the Self-Esteem Controversy. *Educational Leadership,* 49(1), 25-30.

[16] Reynolds, M. (1992). Personal Communication.

[17] Price, N. (1991, Fall) A Poet Inside. *IN*Source Reports.* South Bend, IN: Indiana Resource Center for Families with Special Needs.

[18] Schaffner, C.B.& Buswell, B.E. (1989). *Breaking Ground: Ten Families Building Opportunities Through Integration.* Colorado Springs: PEAK Parent Center, Inc.; Vandercook, T. & York, J. (1989). A Team Approach to Program Development and Support. In J. York, T. Vandercook, C. MacDonald, S. Wolff (Eds.) *Strategies for Full Inclusion.* Minneapolis: University of Minnesota, Institute on Community Integration.

[19] Forest, M. & Lusthaus, E. (1989). Promoting Educational Quality for All Students. In S. Stainback, W. Stainback, & M. Forest (Eds.), *Educating All Students in the Mainstream of Regular Education.* Baltimore: Paul H. Brookes Publishing Co.

[20] Biklen, D. (1992). *Schooling Without Labels: Parents, Educators, and Inclusive Education.* Philadelphia: Temple University Press.

[21] Biklen, D. (1992). *Schooling Without Labels: Parents, Educators, and Inclusive Education.* Philadelphia: Temple University Press.

[22] Quick, D. (1991). Personal Communication.

[23] Dillard, B. (1992). Personal Communication.

[24] Buswell, M.W. (1992). Personal Communication.

[25] Bartolo, M. (1991). Personal Communication.

[26] Bartolo, M. (1991). Personal Communication.

[27] Schaffner, R.L. (1991). Personal Communication.

[28] Miller, J. (1991). Personal Communication.

[29] Buswell, M.W. (1992). Personal Communication.

PERSONAL REFLECTIONS